LA TRAVIATA

Opera in Three Acts

Music by
Giuseppe Verdi

Libretto by
FRANCESCO MARIA PIAVE

English Version by
RUTH and THOMAS MARTIN

Ed. 2420

G. SCHIRMER, Inc.

DISTRIBUTED BY

HAL•LEONARD®
CORPORATION
7777 W. BLUEMOUND RD. P.O. BOX 13819 MILWAUKEE, WI 53213

Photograph of G. Verdi, signed and inscribed to
Gustav Schirmer, founder of the house

Note

G. SCHIRMER, INC.

LA TRAVIATA

If all male actors, both working and unemployed, were to cast their ballots for the star rôle they should prefer to play, it is safe to say that an absolute plurality would go for Hamlet. Performers of every theatrical persuasion, even actresses donning male attire, have at some time in their careers dreamed of appearing in this great part, which conveys so many shades of meaning to divers sectors of the public. If the same type of vote were taken among the ladies, there might be less unanimity of choice. Some might go for the flamboyant splendors of Shakespeare's Cleopatra, others for the craggy strength of his Lady Macbeth, still others for the neurotic intensity of Ibsen's Hedda Gabler; but it would be reasonable to predict a majority for one rôle which seems to have fascinated all actresses since February 2, 1852, when "La Dame aux Camélias" by Alexandre Dumas the Younger was first given in Paris, at the Théâtre des Vaudevilles: Marguerite Gautier. It is surely no accident that two performers with such widely different approaches and techniques as Sarah Bernhardt and Eleonora Duse should both have made this part their own; and that, on the screen, an actress equally individual and arresting, Greta Garbo, should have brought still another quality of creation to the rôle. But not only these great stars remain identified with the part. Other leading actresses have been legion in this most famous of nineteenth-century plays, known to English-speaking audiences as "Camille" and transformed by Verdi, together with his librettist, Francesco Maria Piave, into the opera La Traviata.

It is generally forgotten that, before ending at the footlights, "La Dame aux Camélias" began life as a novel in 1848. Written by a practically unknown author of twenty-four (the reputation of his father, creator of The Three Musketeers and The Count of Monte Cristo, helped not at all in the young man's thorny career), this romance — based on the life story of a young courtesan named Alphonsine Plessis, known more euphoniously as Marie Duplessis, who died of consumption in 1847, at the age of twenty-three — created an immediate stir in Paris. It was dramtized by the author in the following year; but, owing to the censorship which seems to have been the plague of all Europe in this era, it went unproduced until the beginning of 1852 and then reached the stage only through the personal intervention of the Duc de Morny, the power behind the throne of Napoleon III, who had become Emperor of the French in the previous year.

Attracted to the French theater and what it had to offer by way of material for operatic plots, Verdi had already adapted two well-known plays by Victor Hugo to the Italian musical stage — "Hernani (which simply changed its spelling, in transplantation, to Ernani) and "Le Roi s'amuse (known in operatic form as Rigoletto) — before turning to Dumas' "La Dame aux Camélias" in the year that followed its Paris premiere. He is said to have seen the play in performance and been deeply stirred. In any event, he had already signed a contract to provide a new opera for the important Teatro Fenice in Venice; and it was there, on March 6, 1853, that *La Traviata,* its text based on the Dumas tragi-comedy, was first given.

The opening night of this opera was an utter failure. History tells us that, in the final act, when the overly plump Violetta of the evening, Mme. Salvini-Donatelli, was pronounced by her stage physician to be wasting away, the Venetian audience gave vent to howls of laughter. Other inadequacies of direction, especially the handling of the dancers in the ballroom scene, are said to have aroused derision. Verdi, with the uncompromising directness that was to mark his entire professional life, wrote to his young disciple Muzio on the day after the performance: "Dear Emanuele: '*Traviata*' last night — a fiasco. Was it my fault or the singers'? . . . Time will tell."

A glance at the period in which the dramatic action was set may perhaps explain more readily than any obesity on the part of the soprano (after all, this is not rare in opera) why the work failed so dismally. The premiere was given *in modern dress.* Verdi, in the eyes of his conservatively minded public, had dared to draw them out of their plumed and bewigged Never Never Land into contemporary times, bringing them face to face with situations and emotions that might arise in their own lives. This was The Unforgivable, since — in buying his card of admission, even today — the opera goer also purchases a token round trip to the Middle Ages, if not to the moon. Verdi's audience wanted not realism but ritual remoteness. And so *La Traviata* was taken off the boards after two performances. Fourteen months later — May 6, 1854 — the work was revived, once more in Venice but at a different theater, the San Benedetto, by an admirer of Verdi named Antonio Gallo. The composer had revised his score only slightly; the opera was, to practically every intent, the same as before; but this time, costumes and scenery were set back two hundred years, and the audience loved it. It may also be noted that Mme. Salvini-Donatelli had been replaced by a more believable prima donna. The success of this newly mounted version spread throughout Italy, then to all foreign countries where seasons of opera were regularly given, reaching the United States (New York) in December, 1856. The work's public appeal has continued undiminished across the years. Ironically, its scenery and costumes — as mounted in our times — are set in the Paris of Marie Duplessis: the 1840's.

The original play by Dumas is in five acts, the opera by Verdi in three. This spacing of *La Traviata* causes some confusion, because Act Two of the opera — which contains two ample scenes — is rarely, if ever, given as a unit. Both scenes are customarily separated from one another by a full-length intermission, thus becoming in production Acts Two and Three; and the final act of the opera is consequently numbered Four. Such is international tradition. In consulting catalogues of recorded music for the orchestral preludes to the first and last acts of *La Traviata,* the music lover may be puzzled at finding what he knows as the introduction to Act Four in the opera house listed as part of Act Three (the discs all follow the numbering of the original score). This confusion will be compounded by his consulting the score itself, unless he remembers that both scenes of Act Two have grown apart into separate acts in their own right. Actually, Verdi and his librettist Piave adapted and compressed four of the five acts in Dumas' play. The episode they omitted altogether (Act Two in "La Dame aux Camélias") deals with a lovers' quarrel which, though interesting for the light it sheds on Marguerite Gautier's inner force, had to be abandoned for the sake of over-all operatic pacing and unity.

The title of Dumas' work — the reportorial "Lady of the Camellias" — has, in the opera, been changed to the moralizing *La Traviata* ("She Who Has Gone Astray" . . . or, less literally, "The Transgressor"). The names of the characters, too, have almost all been altered. Marguerite Gautier, when set to music, becomes Violetta Valery; the impetuous hero, Armand Duval, grows into Alfredo Germont; his father, Georges, into Giorgio Germont; the vulgar, good-natured Olympe is reborn as Flora Bervoix; Armand's rival for the affections of Marguerite, Baron Varville, is now Baron Douphol. And so on with most of the other characters except for Gaston, who remains the same, and Nanine, the maid, who seems near enough as Annina.

Name-changing, however, is minor alongside the transformations in style, atmosphere and structure that mark the differences between the play and the opera. It can by no means be said that *La Traviata* represents all along the line a consistent improvement over "La Dame aux Camélias," and that the play should be abandoned in favor of its musical counterpart. Those who love the theater and can resist the dazzle of opera will find many debatable pages in the transition. The greatest loss is from the standpoint of characterization, and it has to do with the group of friends who surround Marguerite Gautier: the raffish hangers-on of the Parisian demi-monde, witty, congenial, corrupt, exposed in their hollowness by the playwright, yet never condemned by him. A case in point comes in the final act when Marguerite, ill and desperately out of funds, lends almost half of her remaining money to Prudence, a grasping shopkeeper friend who has been out on the town buying too many New Years' presents. In the opera — where there is no Prudence — Violetta sentimentally bids her maid distribute the dwindling money to poor people in the streets at Carnival time. Then there are all sorts of ingenious touches in Dumas that throw additional light on Gaston, a sympathetic rake; Olympe, a kept woman of kind heart but brassy assurance; Baron Varville, a convincing and ultimately terrible adversary of Armand. In the opera, this group of subordinates, along with the Marquis d'Obigny and Doctor Grenvil, takes its place with Violetta and Alfredo at the supper table of the opening act; but only in their few solo lines do they differ from the choristers who surround them. Dramatically, they show no profile. Verdi was to wait for another nine years, until the masterfully sketched tavern scene in *La Forza del Destino,* before he succeeded in drawing secondary characters sharply from life.

The really fundamental differences between play and opera, however, come in the climaxes . . . and here it is less a matter of opposing tastes than of innate cleavages between the two forms. The spoken drama is, by nature, terse; opera, lyrical and expansive. At the end of the scene in the country house at Auteuil, Armand, after discovering what he believes to be Marguerite's faithlessness, falls overcome in the arms of his father and . . . curtain. In the opera, the father sings an extended aria, *Di Provenza il mar,* urging his son to take a rest cure in the south of France. Again, as the wonderfully dramatic gambling episode comes to an end with Armand contemptuously throwing the money at the feet of Marguerite and, in turn, being challenged by the Baron to a duel . . . curtain. In the opera, Verdi has Alfredo's father turn up at this moment, as a sort of benign gate-crasher and pontificate over his son's behavior in a long, drawn-out finale. This same peripatetic parent reappears — obviously for musical and not dramatic purposes — in Violetta's death scene, where his presence is not recorded in the original play. Indeed, the shock strength of the father's part in the drama arises from the fact that he is seen only once. The influence which he sets in motion persists through the rest of the work.

These are, of course, the debits or, more conservatively put, the controversial aspects of the transition from play to opera. What then, in spite of these, is the nature of the hold which *La Traviata* exerts over audiences of every description? One would answer without hesitation that the strength of the opera lies in its sustained lyricism, sounded from the very first notes of the prelude, its melancholy savor shot through with a musk that lingers uniquely. If the character of Violetta seems foreshortened (none of the wit associated with Marguerite Gautier remains, and her economic status — assured through most of the play by the absent but always generous Duc de Mauriac — grows rather cloudy), the result, musically, by condensation on the literary front, is more concentrated and moving than might otherwise have been possible. Verdi, with the sure instinct of the operatic master, has seized upon several terse moments in the play and expanded them into incomparable passages of melody. For example, Violetta's superb scene and aria, *Ah fors'è lui,* are barely hinted at in the original play. Only in the opera, do the emotional possibilities of this scene come into full bloom. And in a single phrase, Violetta's passionate *Amami, Alfredo!,* sung just before the lovers' parting in Act Two, Verdi has captured all the romantic essence — stripped of Gallic superstructure — to be found in the original play. In fact, he has gone beyond it in intensity. The gambling scene, too, despite the interpolated ballet and chorus of gypsies, which have nothing whatever to do with Dumas' plot, contains an ominous, throbbing quality in its finer moments which illumine certain inner meanings of the drama; and the entire last act, even with the contrived return of the elder Germont, is a music drama *in parvo.* The Violetta who emerges in the death scene is inevitably different, more florid, more rhetorical than the thoroughly modern woman created for us by Dumas; but, in compensation, she bears a haunting musical quality that ranks high in Verdi's total output.

The heart of the opera lies in the touching encounter between Violetta and the elder Germont, which closely parallels the scene in the play. Here Verdi surpasses the original by the disturbing, oppressive rhythms in the orchestra which seem to close in upon the heroine, marking with such pathos the hopelessness of her situation. As she consents to give up Alfredo and says to his father, *Imponete (Tell me what to do)*, a palpitating figure is heard in the strings, *pizzicato*, fitting between disjointed phrases of the conversation, increasing always in intensity, which might well suggest the beating of a troubled heart. In fact, this entire tableau, culminating in Violetta's *Amami, Alfredo!*, sounds a note of lyric drama, of intimate — almost chamber — opera that sets it apart from the rest of Verdi's work, save for certain equally fragile episodes in his final stage piece, *Falstaff*. And thus *La Traviata*, through its varied emotional scheme, can appeal to a very broad public, from young music lovers thrilling to its melodies for the first time to veteran opera goers, still unsated, who have relished its bitter-sweet tunes these many years.

NOTES ON PERFORMANCE

La Traviata is essentially a prima donna's opera. It stands or falls by the performance of the singer who assumes the part of Violetta. Since Verdi fashioned this rôle for a type of artist broadly equipped emotionally and vocally, some confusion exists today about the kind of voice best qualified to do it justice. There can be no clear-cut answer, since this opera, in its many-faceted approach to Violetta, contains passages ideally suited in themselves to specialized lyric, dramatic or coloratura sopranos. Yet, when these passages are taken in context, it will be realized that a voice of exceptionally generous color and over-all flexibility is required. Many famous coloratura sopranos have been heard in concert performances of Violetta's brilliant *Sempre libera*, which ends the first act, but how many of these singers can sustain a performance of the entire part? Very few. Of assorted names in the lexicons, only those of Tetrazzini, Hempel and Galli-Curci come to mind; and none in our own time. The fact remains that *Sempre libera* is not coloratura at all, but fioritura — the grafting of florid passages onto a body of music that is essentially lyric or dramatic, not for display purposes but for heightened expressivity. Here Violetta, as yet afraid to commit herself to the love of one man for fear of rejection, decides — only later to reverse herself — that she will slip back into the vortex of the Parisian demi-monde from which she has been yearning to escape. As she refers to the false glitter of this world, a hectic, feverish coloration appears in music basically suited to a lyric or even a dramatic voice. Foremost among the dramatic sopranos who have sung the part stand the names of Rosa Ponselle and Claudia Muzio; the lyric artists have included Lucrezia Bori, Bidu Sayao, Licia Albanese, Renata Tebaldi, Maria Callas, Eleanor Steber, Anna Moffo, Dorothy Kirsten and Victoria de Los Angeles.

On occasion, the *Sempre libera* is taken down half a tone, from A-flat major to G. This alteration aside, there are no performance changes of any kind in the first act. None occurs in the third, either, or in the fourth, save that the second strophe of Violetta's aria, *Addio del passato* (pages 200 to 201 of the Schirmer piano vocal score) is customarily omitted. The two final measures of the aria are joined to the ending of the first stanza. Some smaller companies dispense with the band effects off-stage in the first and last act, "cueing" them — for economy reasons — into the orchestra pit; but any self-respecting, financially solvent organization will have these effects performed in the wings, as written, with an incalculable gain in over-all dramatic and musical color.

It is the second act, the scene at Violetta's country home, which is most often subjected to changes; and since conductors in the big opera houses seem to prefer making their own cuts in this act, rather than following any set international traditions, there can be no completely standard list of alterations. The *cabaletta* for Alfredo, which follows upon his well-known *Del miei bollenti spiriti*, is almost always omitted (this cut runs from the Allegro on page 74 of the Schirmer piano vocal score until the Allegro on page 81). In the big duet between Violetta and the elder Germont, it is customary to leave out twelve measures on page 100, beginning with Violetta's *Conosca il sacrifizio* and proceeding to where she takes these words for a second time. Since the phrase omitted (for Violetta alone) anticipates musically and textually the same melody as sung by her in ensemble with Germont, there is no loss involved but, on the contrary, a desirable tightening-up. On page 110, the brief conversation between Alfredo and the messenger who hands him a letter from Violetta is practically always omitted, the cut beginning with the messenger's opening words, *Il signor Germont?* and ending with his final phrase, *mi diede questo scritto*. The letter is usually (but not invariably) proffered in silence by a stage butler.

The close of this scene in the country brings a big alteration on which leading authorities are not always in agreement. Germont's cabaletta, *No, no udrai rimproveri*, which follows his celebrated *Di Provenza il mar*, is universally suppressed; but the cut beginning at the top of page 115, after Germont's appeal to Alfredo, *Nè rispondi d'un padre all' affetto?*, is taken in various ways. The one in widest use is appended here. Germont's appeal closes with two altered notes leading into the cut, which runs all the way to page 120, measure 7, whence everything further until the end of the scene (fourteen measures in all) is thrown into D-flat major. The reason for the long cut is obvious — to speed up the sense of drama and of climax. But the cause of the transposition? The world of opera is calculating: to give the baritone a high A-flat with which to show off his topmost range.

Robert Lawrence

Page 114 (bottom) . . . . . . to . . . Page 120 (middle)

x

Cast of Characters

VIOLETTA VALERY . . . . Soprano

FLORA BERVOIX . . . . Mezzo-Soprano

ANNINA . . . . Soprano

ALFREDO GERMONT . . . . Tenor

GIORGIO GERMONT, his father . . . . Baritone

GASTONE, Viscount of Letorieres . . . . Tenor

BARON DOUPHOL . . . . Baritone

MARQUIS D'OBIGNY . . . . Bass

DOCTOR GRENVIL . . . . Bass

GIUSEPPE, servant to Violetta . . . . Tenor

SERVANT TO FLORA . . . . Bass

MESSENGER . . . . Bass

Friends of Violetta and Flora, Matadors, Picadors, Gypsies, Servants, etc.

Time: About 1850.

The action takes place in and near Paris.

Index

ACT I

La Traviata.
Act I.
Nº 1. Prelude.

GIUSEPPE VERDI.

44878c

Nº 2. "Dell'invito trascorsa è già l'ora".

Introduction.

(A salon in Violetta's house. In the rear is a door which leads into another room; there are two other doors at the sides. At left, is a fireplace over which is a mirror. In the center, a table is lavishly set.

Allegro brillantissimo e molto vivace.

Violetta, seated on a divan, is conversing with the Doctor and other friends; others welcome arriving guests, among whom are the Baron, and Flora on the arm of the Marquis.)

4

(They sit down. Violetta sits between Alfred and Gaston; Flora sits down opposite her, between the Baron and the Marquis. The others sit down at their pleasure.)

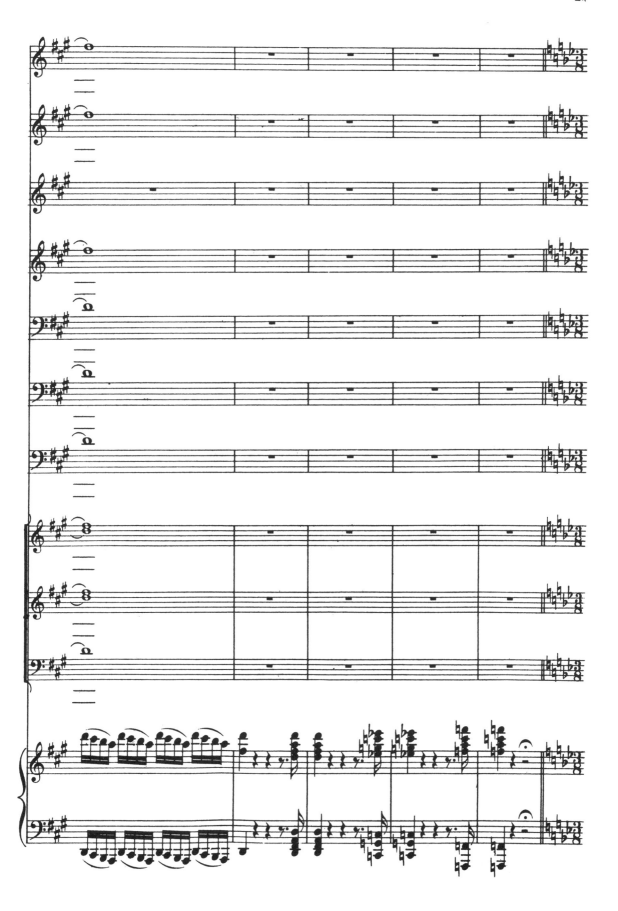

Nº 3. "Libiamo ne' lieti calici,,.

Drinking-song.

Nº 4. "Un dì felice, eterea."

Valse and Duet.

(*They start for the ballroom; Violetta has a sudden fit of weakness.*)

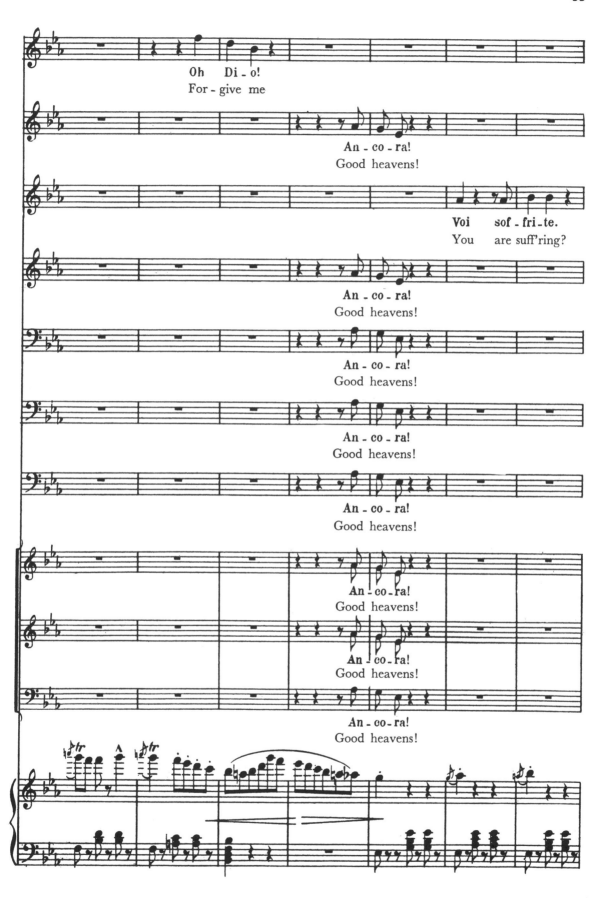

48

44878

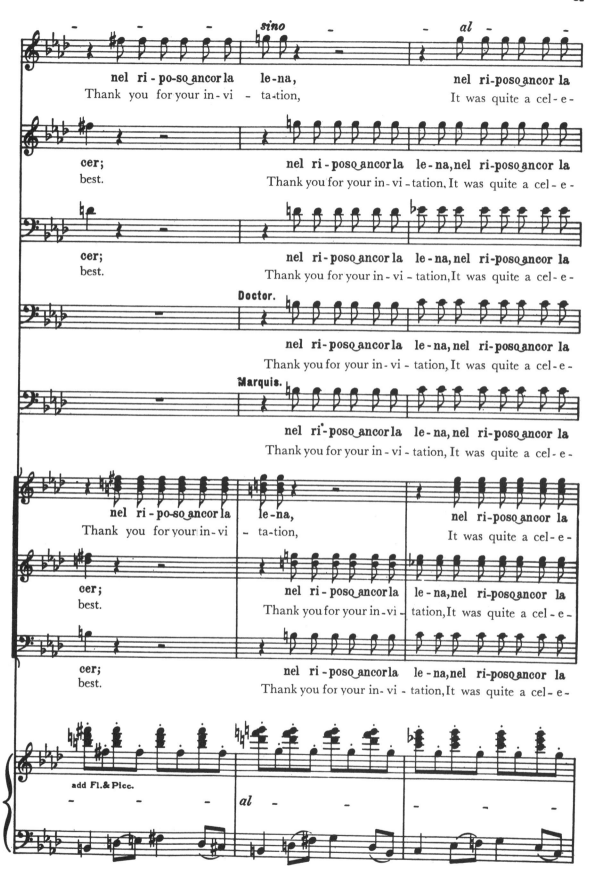

le-na si ri-tempri per go-der,
bra-tion and the hours seemed to fly.

sì, per go-der, sì, nel ri-po-so ancor la
We thank you once a-gain and say good-bye, We

le-na si ri-tempri per go-der,
bra-tion and the hours seemed to fly.

sì, per go-der, sì, nel ri-po-so ancor la
We thank you once a-gain and say good-bye, We

le-na si ri-tempri per go-der,
bra-tion and the hours seemed to fly.

sì, per go-der, sì, nel ri-po-so ancor la
We thank you once a-gain and say good-bye, We

le-na si ri-tempri per go-der,
bra-tion and the hours seemed to fly.

sì, per go-der, sì, nel ri-po-so ancor la
We thank you once a-gain and say good-bye, We

le-na si ri-tempri per go-der,
bra-tion and the hours seemed to fly.

sì, per go-der, sì, nel ri-po-so ancor la
We thank you once a-gain and say good-bye, We

le-na si ri-tem-pri per go-der,
bra-tion and the hours seemed to fly.

sì, per go-der, sì, nel ri-poso ancor la
We thank you once a-gain and say good-bye, We

le-na si ri-tem-pri per go-der,
bra-tion and the hours seemed to fly.

sì, per go-der, sì, nel ri-poso ancor la
We thank you once a-gain and say good-bye, We

le-na si ri-tem-pri per go-der,
bra-tion and the hours seemed to fly.

sì, per go-der, sì, nel ri-poso ancor la
We thank you once a-gain and say good-bye, We

Vln.

Tutti

(All the guests leave.)

le - na si ri - tem-pri per go - der.
thank you once a - gain and say good-bye.

№ 6. "Ah, fors'è lui che l'anima.„

Recit. and Air.

*A cut is usually made from here to page 62, line 4.

66

44878

End of Act I.

44878

Act II.

(A country house near Paris. A room on the ground floor. In the rear, facing the audience, is a mantelpiece; on it a mirror and a clock between two glass doors leading into the garden. Two other doors, right and left. Chairs, small tables and writing utensils.)

№ 7. "De' miei bollenti spiriti.„

Recit. and Air.

(Alfred enters in hunting clothes)

lu - ne dac - chè la mia Vio - let-ta a - gi per me la - sciò, do - vi - zie, a -
read-y Since she de-sert-ed Pa-ris, Ab-an-don-ing, for my sake, Her pleas-ures, her

mo - ri, e le pom-po - se fe-ste, ov', a-gli_o-maggi av-vez-za, ve-dea schia-vo cias-
lov-ers, And all those bril-liant par-ties Where, like a queen of beau-ty, She reigned o-ver the

Andante.

cun di sua bel-lez-za. Ed or con-ten-ta in que-sti a-me-ni luo-ghi tut-to scor-da per
hearts of countless ad - mir - ers. Now she is hap-py in this de-light-ful coun-try, Liv-ing on - ly for

Adagio.

me. Qui pres-so_a lei io ri - na - scer mi sen-to, e dal
me. With her be - side me my life __ has new mean-ing; And re -

sof-fio d'amor ri-ge-ne-ra-to scor-do ne'gau-di suo-i tut - to il pas-
born through her love And her de - vo-tion, Now I may live en - joy-ing hap - pi-ness true and

Andante.(♩ = 60)

sa - to.
last - ing.

pp Str. pizz.

44878

(He rushes off.)

Nº 8. "Pura siccome un angelo.„

Recit. and Duet.

Andante piuttosto mosso (♪ = 96)

parlante

Violetta.

Bella voi sie-te, e gio-vi-ne; col tempo— Ah più non di - te— v'in-ten-do, me impos-
You are so young yet and beau-ti-ful; A new love No more, I beg you! What-ev-er you may

Germont.

si - bi - le, lui so-lo a-mar vo-gli-o. Sia
say to me I nev-er could love an - oth - er... That

pu - re, ma vo - lu - bi - le so-
may be. But who knows how long his

ven - te è l'uom. Gran Di - o! Un dì, quan-do le
love will last? O heav - en! The day when grace and

Violetta. (startled)   Germont. *con semplicità*

ve - ne - ri il tem-po a-vrà fu - ga - te, fia pre-sto il te - dio a
love-li - ness, The bloom of youth have fad - ed, Your pres - ent state of

sor-ge-re__ Che sa-rà al-lor? Pen-sa - te! Per voi non a-vran
hap-pi-ness, Where will it be? Con-sid - er! You would not have the

bal-sa-mo i più so-a-vi af-fet - ti, poi-chè dal ciel non
sol-ace Of sweet-er deep af-fec - tion, For love can-not en-

Violetta.

È ve-ro! è
It's true,__ it's

fu - ro-no__ tai no - di be-ne-det - ti. Ah
dure__ With-out__ the__ bless - ing of the Lord a - bove, I

Fl. Ob. & Cl.

Str. arco

ve - ro!
true!__

dun - que, dun - que sper-da-si tal so - gno se - dut -
beg you to a - ban - don Such vain and hope - less

voi che far pos-s'i - o? che far pos-s'i - o? o ge-ne-
way can I re-pay you, re-pay you ev - er The debt I

ro - - - - - sa! Mor -
owe _____ you? I'll

Violetta (*turning to him*)

Allegro moderato. (♩=108)

rò! mor-rò! la mia me-mo-ri-a non fi - a ch'ei ma-le-di-ca, se
die! And then let him re-mem-ber me With-out bit-ter ma-le-dic-tion; Re-

Str. pizz. Cl. & Fag. sustain.

morendo **Germont.**

le mie pene or - ri - bi - li vi sia chi almen gli di - ca. No, ge-ne-ro-sa,
veal my hope-less suf-fer-ing, My an-guish and af-flic - tion. No, you will live, and

vi - ve - re e lie - ta __ voi do-vre - te. Mer-cè di queste la-grime dal
hap-pi-ly A joy - ous __ fate ac-cord-ed; What you have done for all __ of us, By

44878

Nº 9. "Dammi tu forza, o cielo."
Recitative.

44878

Nº 10. "Di Provenza il mar, il suol."

Recit. and Aria.

110

44878

dolce

Di Pro-ven-za il mar, il suol chi dal
Can your heart be dead and cold To all

cor ti can-cel-lò? chi dal cor ti can-cel-lò di Pro-ven-za il mar, il suol? Al na-
mem-o-ries of home, Of the land you loved to roam In your childhood days of old? What de-

tio ful-gen-te sol qual de-sti-no ti fu-rò? Qual de-sti-no ti fu-rò al na-
lu-sion could it be That has made you break your ties With your sun-ny na-tive skies, And the

tio fulgente sol? Oh ram-men-ta pur nel duol ch'i-vi gio-ja a te bril-lò, e che
blue and shining sea? Now re-mem-ber what you owe To all those who hold you dear. In their

pa-ce co-là sol su te splende-re ancor può, e che pa-ce co-là sol su te
midst you always know Their af-fec-tion is sin-cere, And the peace of long a-go Will re-

con forza

ppp rall.

splendere ancor può. Dio mi gui-do! Dio mi gui-do! Dio mi gui-do!
turn when they are near. God wills it so! God wills it so! God wills it so!

Fl. Picc.
Oh. Cl.

p Str.

allarg.

A il tuo
From the

morendo

Str.

dolciss.

marc.

pp

vecchio ge-ni-tor tu non sai quan-to sof-frì, tu non sai quan-to sof-frì il tuo
time you went away, Of our joy we were bereaved? Your poor father's heart was grieved And he

dolce

marc.

vecchio ge-ni-tor! Te lon-ta-no, di squal-lor il suo tet-to si co-prì, il suo
suf-fered day by day! I have nev-er ceased to pray That my hopes be not in vain, And that

Wind

pp

pp

tet-to si co-prì, di squal-lo-re, di squal-lor. Ma se al-fin ti tro-vo an-cor, se in me
you would see your way To come home to us a-gain. If at last the gra-cious Lord Has re-

pp

Assai moderato. (♩ = 96)

No, non u - drai rim - pro - ve - ri, co - priam d'o - blio il pas - sa - to; __ l'a - mor che m'ha gui -
Not one re proach shall come from me, Nor shall I ev - er blame you. With love I came to

da - to sa tut - to per - do - nar. Vie - ni i tuoi ca - ri in giu - bi - lo con me ri - ve - dian -
claim you, For - giv - ing all the past. Your dear ones tru - ly long to see Our fam - il - y u -

co - ra, a chi pe - ro fi - no - ra tal gio - ja non ne - gar. Un pa - dre e d u - na
nit - ed; Our wish will be re - quit - ed, When you re - turn at last. Your fath - er and your

suo - ra t'af - fret - ta a con - so - la - re, un pa - dre e d u - na suo - ra t'af - fret - ta a conso -
sis - ter Are wait - ing to con - sole you. With love and un der standing To heal your wounded

lar,   un pa-dre ed u - na suo - - ra, sì, t'af -
past.   Your fath - er and your sis - - - ter are

fret - ta,   ah sì, t'af - fret - ta,   ah sì, t'af - fret - ta a con - so -
wait - ing.   They want to help you   for-get the past, for - get the

DE   **Alfred** *(turns, notices Flora's letter on the table, reads it and exclaims:)*

Ah!   el - l'e al - la fe - sta!   vo - li - si l'of -
Ah,   she went to Flo - ra's . . .   This out - ra - geous

lar!   *colla parte*
past.

(He rushes away, followed by Germont.)

fe - sa a ven - di - car!   Che di - ci?   ah fer - - ma!
shame I will a - venge!   Don't do it!   I beg - - you!

№ 11. "Avrem lieta di maschere la notte.„

Finale

(A richly furnished and illuminated room in Flora's house; a door in the rear and two side doors. At right, more to the foreground, a large gambling table. At left, a table elaborately set with flowers and refreshments. Several chairs and a divan. Flora, the Marquis, the Doctor and other guests enter, conversing.)

(The noise of arriving guests is heard.)

Si-len-zio_ U -
Be qui-et and

vi - di ie - ri an-cor!_ pa - re an fe - li - ci.
saw them both last night. They seemed ver - y hap-py.

_pp_

di - te!_ Giun - go - no gli a - mi - ci.
lis - ten. The par - ty is be - gin-ning.

Giun - go - no gli a - mi - ci.
The par - ty is be - gin-ning.

Giun - go - no gli a - mi - ci.
The par - ty is be - gin-ning.

Wind.
cresc.

ff Tutti.

Nº 12. "Noi siamo zingarelle.,,
Chorus of Gipsies.

(*A group of ladies dressed as gypsies enter; also dancers in gypsy costume.*)

44878

(Flora and the Marquis are re
conciled; he presses her hand.)

Nº 13. "Di Madride noi siam mattadori,,.
Chorus of Spanish Matadors.

(Gaston and other masqueraders, dressed as matadors and picadors, enter briskly from the right.)

co - si al gio - va - ne___ par - lò: Cin - que
Wed him till she was___ o - beyed. "If you

to - ri_in un sol gior - no vo' ve - der_ti_ad at - ter - rar,
kill_ five bulls in one day Then I'll say___ you are a suc - cess!

e, se vin - ci_al tuo___ ri - tor - no ma - no_e cor - ti
If you do_ it, then, next Mon - day, I can prom - ise

vo'___ do - nar. Sì,___ gli dis - se_e il mat - ta - do - re al__ le
I'll say 'yes.'" Said___ Pi - quil - lo: "I___ will do it, That___ will

(The Picadors strike the ground with their staves wherever the sign + occurs.)

gio - stre mo - se il piè; cin - que to - ri, vin - ci - to - re,
not be hard__ for me!" And__ be - fore__ his sweet-heart knew it,

gio - stre mo - se il piè; cin - que to - ri, vin - ci - to - re,
not be hard for me!" And__ be - fore__ his sweet-heart knew it,

sul - l'a - re - na e - gli sten - dè, cin - que to - ri,
He__ had done__ it, one__ two three! Five__ bulls dead,__ and

sul - l'a - re - na e - gli sten - dè, cin - que to - ri,
He__ had done__ it, one__ two three! Five__ bulls dead,__ and

vin - ci - to - re, sul - l'a - re - na e - gli sten - dè.
noth - ing to it, What a might - y man__ was he!

vin - ci - to - re, sul - l'a - re - na e - gli sten - dè.
noth - ing to it, What a might - y man__ was he!

138 Matadors and Picadors.

44878

(The men unmask. Some disperse, while others begin to play at the gambling table.)

Nº 14. "Alfredo! Voi!„
Continuation of Finale

(Alfred enters seemingly unconcerned.)

44878

vol - to! bra-vo! *(aloud)* Or via, giuocar si può.
bar - rassed, bra-vo! And now, let's have a game!

vol - to! bra-vo! Or via, giuocar si può.
bar - rassed, bra-vo! And now, let's have a game!

vol - to! bra-vo! Or via, giuocar si può.
bar - rassed, bra-vo! And now, let's have a game!

vol - to! bra-vo! *(aloud)* Or via, giuocar si può.
bar - rassed, bra-vo! And now, let's have a game!

vol - to! bra-vo! Or via, giuocar si può.
bar - rassed, bra-vo! And now, let's have a game!

vol - to! bra-vo! Or via, giuocar si può.
bar - rassed, bra-vo! And now, let's have a game!

ff

Allegro agitato.

(Gaston deals; Alfred and the others are playing.

ppp Str. & Cl.

Violetta enters on the arm

of the Baron. Flora goes to meet them.)

tar - di la ri - vin - ci-ta. Al giuo - co che vor - re - te.
we shall see who's luck - y then. What-ev - er is your pleas-ure.

Baron.

Se - guiam gli a - mi - ci
Let's fol-low the oth-ers.

Alfred.

po - scia Sa - rò qual bra - me - re - te.
lat - er...I'll be at your dis - pos-al.

(They leave the room.)

Baron *(from a distance)*

An - diam.
Till then.

An - diam.
Till then.

col - po vi tor - ri - a, un sol col - po vi tor - ri - a col - l'a -
blow I would de - prive you, With one blow I would de - prive you Of your

Violetta.

man - te jl pro - tet - to - re _ V'at - ter - ri - sce tal scia - gura? Ma s'ei
lov - er and pro - tect - or! Does that pros - pect make you trem - ble? But if

Wind sustain

fos - se l'uc - ci - so - re! ec - co l'u - ni - ca sven - tu - ra ch'io pa -
he in - stead should kill you That would be the one mis - for - tune I would

Alfred.

ven - to a me fa - ta - le. La mia mor - te! _ che ven -
dread a - bove all oth - ers. If he killed me? Why should

Violetta. Alfred.

ca - le? Deh, par - ti - te _ e sul - l'i - stante. Par - ti -
you care? Do not stay here! De - part this in - stant! I shall

233

rò, ma giu-ra in - nan-te che do - vun-que se - gui - ra - i, se-gui-

go; but not un - til You prom-ise on your word of hon-or To re-

237

Violetta.

Ah no, giam-ma - i.

Ah no, I can-not!

Va, sciagu-

rai i pas-si mie - i.

turn___ to the coun-try.

No, giam-ma - i?

So you can not?

You must be-

241

ra - to! scorda un no - me ch'è in-fa - ma - to, va, mi la-scia sul mo-

lieve me and for-get me. Go and leave me at this mo-ment. I im-

245

men-to___ di fug-gir - ti un giu - ra - men-to sa-cro io

plore you, for I gave my sol - emn word That I will

265

Flora.

Ne ap - pel - laste? che vo - le - te?   Alfred *(indicating Violetta)*
What has hap-pened? Well, what is it?

Questa don - - na co - no -
Do you all _____ here know this

Gaston.

Ne ap - pel - laste? che vo - le - te?
What has hap-pened? Well, what is it?

Chorus.

Ne ap - pel - la-ste? che vo - le - te?
What has hap-pened? Well, what is it?

Ne ap - pel - la-ste? che vo - le - te?
What has hap-pened? Well, what is it?

Baron, Doctor and Marquis with BASS.

Str.   Vl.

p   dim.   Cello

Fag Ophicleide & D.-b.

272

Violetta. *(softly to Alfred)*   Flora.

Chi! Vio - let-ta?   (Ah! ta-ci.)   No.
Who? Vio-let-ta?   Don't say it!   No!

sce-te?   Che fa - ces - - se non sa - pe-te?
wom-an?   What she did, _____ you do not know yet?

Chi! Vio - let-ta?   No.
Who? Vio-let-ta?   No!

Chi! Vio - let-ta?   No.
Who? Vio-let-ta?   No!

Chi! Vio - let-ta?   No.
Who? Vio-let-ta?   No!

ff   Tutti.

44878

301

(With furious contempt he throws a purse at Violetta's feet. She faints into the arms of Flora.)

(At this moment Germont enters.)

Continuation of Finale

168

44878

186

44878

(Germont draws Alfred with him. The Baron follows him. Violetta is led by Flora into another room. The others disperse.)

End of the Second Act.

Act III.

(The bedroom of Violetta. In the rear is a bed with curtains half drawn and a window with closed shutters. Near the bed is a small table on which is a decanter of water and several medicines. In the center, a dressing table near a sofa. Further away is another piece of furniture on which a lamp is burning dimly, also several chairs and other pieces. A door is at left. In front, is a fire-place with a fire burning.

Nᵒ 16. "Addio del passato.„

Recit. and Aria.

Violetta is asleep on the bed. Annina, sitting in a chair near the fireplace, has also fallen asleep.)

Violetta (*awakening*)

An-ni-na!
An-ni-na?

Dor-mi-vi? po-ve-ret-ta!
I woke you? You were sleep-ing.

Annina (*rising, confused*)

Co-man-da-te?
Did you call me?

Sì, per-do-
Yes, please for-

Recit.

(*Annina gives her a glass of water.*)

Dam-mi d'ac-qua un sor-so.
May I have some wa-ter.

Os-
And

na-te.
give me.

pp

Vl. divided.

(Annina opens the shutters and looks out onto the street.)

(She tries to rise but falls back. Then, supported by Annina, she goes slowly toward the sofa. The Doctor arrives in time to assist her.)

corpo, ma tranquilla ho l'alma. Mi confortò ier sera un pio mi-
suff'ring, my mind is peaceful. A priest heard my confession And brought me

ni-stro, ah! re-li-gi-o-ne è sollievo ai sof-fe-ren-ti. E questa
comfort. Ah, re-li-gion lightens and consoles the troubled spirit. How did you

Doctor.

Violetta.

not-te? Eb-bi tranquillo il son-no. Co-rag-gio a-dun-que
sleep? Calm-ly, with-out a-wak-ing. Then do not wor-ry,

Doctor.

Violetta.

la con-va-le-scen-za non è lon-ta-na. Oh! la bu-gia pie-
You are on the way to con-va-les-cence. You say that out of

to-sa ai me-di-ci è con-ces-sa! Ad-di-o, a più
kind-ness Be-cause you want to cheer me! Good-by then, till this

Doctor. (*pressing her hand*)

(The Doctor leaves. Annina escorts him.)

Violetta. Annina (softly and quickly) Doctor.

tar-di! Non vi scor-da-te. Co-me va, si-gno-re? La ti-si non le ac-
eve-ning. You won't for get me? How is she, Doc-tor? I think that by to-

(Exit) (returning to
Annina. Violetta

cor-da che po-che o - re. Or fa-te
night it will all be o - ver. You must take

Vl. divided.

and attempting
to cheer her) Violetta. Annina.

cor. Gior-no di fe-sta è questo? Tut-ta Pa-ri-gi im-paz-za è car-ne-va-le.
heart. Is-n't to - day a holiday? Paris is wild with excitement, Because it's Carnival.

Str.

Violetta.

Ah nel co-mun tri-pu-dio, sal-lo Id-di-o quanti in-fe-li - ci soffron! Qua-le
And while the crowd re-joic-es, God a-lone knows how man y poor are suf-f'ring! How much

somma v'ha in quello sti-po? Die-ci ne re-ca a' po-ve-ri tu
mon-ey is there left now? Ten of them give to the poor and

Annina (opens a box and counts)

Ven-ti lu-i-gi.
Just twen-ty louis d'ors.

44878

con dolore

stes-sa. Oh mi sa-ran ba-stan-ti! Cer-ca po-scia mie
need-y. Oh, I shall nev-er need it. Will you go for my

Po - co ri - man-vi al-lo-ra.
That will— leave you lit-tle.

(Annina leaves.

let - te - re. Nul-l'oc-cor-rà, sol-le-ci-ta, se puo - i.
let-ters now? I'll be al-right, but try your best to hur - ry.

Ma voi?
But you? . . .

Violetta takes a letter from her bosom and reads in a soft voice.)

Andantino. (♪= 88.)
1st Vl.

"Teneste la pro-messa— La disfida ebbe
"You have kept your promise. The duel took

pp

pp

1st & 2d Vl., 2 Viole
1 'Cello, 1 C.b. trem.

luogo— Il barone fu ferito, però migliora— Alfredo è in stranio suolo. Il vostro sacri-
place—the Baron was wounded, but he is recovering . . . Alfred is on foreign soil. I myself

fizio io stesso gli ho sve - lato. Egli a voi torne-rà pel suo perdono; io pur ver - rò;
revealed your sacrifice to him. He is returning to beg your forgiveness . . . I will come

(desolately)

Curatevi . . . . mertate un avve - nir migliore. — *Giorgio Germont.,,* È tardi!
with him. May you soon recover and a happier future be yours. George Germont." Too late!

Tutti Str. Cl.
Fag. & Cor.

(she rises) *(She looks into the mirror.)*

At - ten - do, at - ten - do, nè a me giun-gon ma - i! Oh co - me son mu-
I wait-ed and wait-ed But my days are num-bered. Ah, how my ill-ness

ta - ta! Ma il Dot - to - re a spe-rar pu - re m'e-sor-ta! Ah, con tal
changed me! But the doc-tor gave me hope of re - - cov'ry . . . Ah, with such an

Adagio. Andante mosso. ($\,$= 50.) dolente e **pp**

mor - bo o - gni speranza è mor - ta! Ad-
ill-ness I know that all is hope - less. Fare-

44878

Nº 17. "Largo al quadrupede.,,

Bacchanal Chorus.

(From the street the singing of a merry carnival crowd is heard.)

(The sound fades away.)

Nº 18. "Parigi, o cara, noi lasceremo.,,
Recit. and Duet.

44878

dolcissimo a mezza voce.

Pa-ri-gi,o ca-ra, noi la-sce-re-mo, la vi-ta u-ni-ti tra-scor-re-
Noth-ing, my dear - est, shall now re-mind us Of _ all the suf-f'ring we leave be-

stacc. sempre.

re - mo, de' cor-si af-fan - ni com-pen-so a-vra - i, la _ tua sa-
hind us. And far from Pa - ris, far from in-tru - sion, You _ shall re-

f

lu - te ri-fio-ri - rà. So-spi-ro e lu - ce tu _ mi sa-ra - i,
cov - er, free from all care. Liv-ing u - nit - ed in _ sweet se - clu - sion,

f *pp* **Violetta.** *dolce a mezza voce*

tut-to il fu - tu-ro ne ar-ri-de - rà. Pa-ri-gi,o ca - ro, noi la-sce-
Our love will bring us hap-pi-ness to share. Noth-ing, my dear - est, shall now re-

re - mo, la _ vi-ta u-ni - ti tra-scor-re - re-mo, de' cor-si af-
mind us Of _ all the suf-f'ring we _ leave be-hind us. And _ far from

Alfred.

Sì,
Yes.

Nº19."Prendi, quest' è l'immagine.,,
Finale.

a drawer and takes a medallion from it.)

Ah malcau-to ve-gliardo! il mal ch'io fe-ci, o-ra sol ve-do!
How mis guid-ed a fath-er! The wrong I did her Now is ap-par-ent.

Violetta.

Più a me t'ap-pres-sa, a-scol-ta, a-ma-to Al-fre-do:
Come here be-side me and lis-ten, Be-lov-ed Al-fred!

Andante sostenuto. (♩=56) *(to Alfred)*

Prendi, quest'è l'im-ma-gi-ne de'
Dear-est, on this med-al-li-on You

miei pas-sa-ti gior-ni, a ram-men-tar ti
see my past re-sem-blance to keep as a re-

tor-ni co-lei che sì t'a-mò. No, non mor-rai, non
mem-brance Of her who loved you so. You must not die, but

Alfred.

Germont. Ca-ra, su-
Can you for-

44878

*Usually omitted.

*It is customary to omit all singing from here to the end.